Battleship v. Battleship

Task Force 34's Moment of Glory

By J. Lanham Pearson

NIMBLE BOOKS LLC

J. LANHAM PEARSON

ISBN-13: 978-1-934840-40-5

ISBN-10: 1-934840-40-8

Copyright 2008 J. Lanham Pearson

Version 1.0; last saved 2008-05-27.

Nimble Books LLC

1521 Martha Avenue

Ann Arbor, MI 48103-5333

http://www.nimblebooks.com

This book was produced using Microsoft Word 2007 and Adobe Acrobat 8.1. The cover was produced using The Gimp. The cover font, heading fonts and the body text inside the book are in Constantia, designed by John Hudson for Microsoft.

The cover photograph shows the modernized U.S.S. *Iowa,* BB-61, firing her broadside in 1984. This is close to what an observer at Leyte Gulf would have seen in the early morning of October 25 as Task Force 34 engaged Kurita's Center Force.

Contents (including Figures)

Introduction iv
About the Author v
Acknowledgements v
A Brief Background 1
Forming Task 34 2
    Figure 1. *Musashi* down at the bow after air attack, October 24, 1944. 2
    Figure 2. A map from the MacArthur report (overleaf). 4
The Opposing Forces 7
    Figure 3. U.S.S. *New Jersey*, BB-62, at sea in the Pacific, 1944. 8
    Figure 4. Ship Tonnage. 9
    Figure 5. Broadside weight per minute in tons (total all ships with rate of fire included). 9
    Figure 6. Torpedoes. 9
    Figure 7. A Japanese Type 93 "Long Lance" torpedo on display outside U.S. Navy headquarters, Washington, during World War II. 10
    Figure 9. U.S.S. *Iowa*, BB-61, at sea 1944. 11
    Figure 10. Office of Naval Intelligence profile of *Kongo* and *Haruna*, 1941. 14
    Figure 11. U.S.S. *Washington*, BB-56, 1944. 14
    Figure 12. Heavy cruiser *Chikuma* inducing indigestion in U.S. skippers. ... 15
    Figure 13. Destroyer *Shimakaze*, 1943. 16
    Figure 14. U.S.S. *Fletcher*, DD-445, underway off New York, 1942. 17
The Battle 19
    Figure 15. U.S.S. *Alabama*, BB-60, December 1942. 21
The Opening Rounds 21
    Figure 16. *Yamato* under air attack, 1945. 24
The Battle Continues 24
The Cruiser and Destroyer Battle 26
    Figure 17. U.S.S. *Cleveland*, CL-55, under way late 1942. 27
    Figure 18. Battleship *Nagato*, from the George Grantham Bain collection at the Library of Congress. 28
Last Salvos 29
Aftermath 30
BB-67 *Montana*, U.S. Navy Battleship: Why She Matters Today (also from Nimble Books) 33
Colophon 34

INTRODUCTION

Frequently momentous events in history are surrounded by a collection of "what if" propositions. Decisions made by those who were there often become debates in which late-comers suggest what should have been "if." For these decisive moments in history, the passage of time only seems to polarize the positions of the debaters.

A decision, made by Admiral William F. Halsey on October 24th 1944, then the Commander of the United States Navy's Third Fleet, is at the heart of this work. His choice that day was whether to head north, from the area of the invasion beaches off Leyte Gulf in the Philippines, to take advantage of a sighting of the Japanese Fleet's carrier force. If he could close the distance between the two forces, he could once-and-for-all annihilate them.

In the end he decided to take his entire force, including all of his battleships, with him. It is the decision to take all of the battleships along that has undergone debate literally since that day. For also nearing the Leyte beaches were two powerful Japanese fleets, each centered on battleships. One force, entering Surigao Strait, was met by the old battleships of the US Seventh fleet and, in a night action, almost completely destroyed. The other, unchecked by a blocking force, came straight through the San Bernardino Strait and collided head on with an escort carrier support group, who seemingly had no prayer of stopping battleships.

This book doesn't attempt to analyze Halsey's decision. Rather it examines what would have happened if he had decided to employ a plan that he had conceived for just the chance that the Japanese would come through. Halsey had designated several ships to become a blocking force and designated it "Task Force 34." Included in that force were four modern US battleships.

It is here that this book makes its contribution to historical analysis. Indeed, all criticism of the leaders involved aside, this book ponders what would have actually happened if Task Force 34 had been left behind to guard San Bernardino Strait?

ABOUT THE AUTHOR

J. Lanham Pearson grew up in the Chicago, Illinois area, played WWII naval miniatures as a high schooler, and never lost his love for the history of the War in the Pacific. In professional life he is a police commander, serving 30 years with distinction on a metropolitan police force. An amateur historian, he is currently completing a bachelor's degree in management.

ACKNOWLEDGEMENTS

This book is dedicated to my wife Marcy, the love of my life.

I would be remiss if I did not acknowledge some of the assistance I have received in completing this piece.

Parts of this work were originally posted on the Chuck Hawks history page. Chuck was very helpful to me and gave me sound advice during the project. His webpage is a fun read and covers all kinds of oral histories.

http://www.chuckhawks.com/index3.naval_military_history.htm

My wife Marcy and publisher/editor W.F. Zimmerman deserve much of the credit in getting this work in its present form. Thank you both.

J. Lanham Pearson

A Brief Background

On October 20th 1944 US Army troops of the 10th and 24th Corps stormed ashore on the island of Leyte, bringing flesh and steel to finally fulfill Douglass MacArthur's promise of "I shall return." At the time there was no more vital possession of the Japanese Empire, save the home islands themselves. Everything that came to Japan from the south, including most of Japan's oil, had to pass by the Philippines. Leyte was the stepping stone to retaking them.

Hoarding their great navy to the last, the Japanese leaders had drawn a prophetic line around the Philippines. They would commit their navy, all of it, in a desperate fight to prevent the United States from retaking that vital land mass. Having lost the air superiority battle both over land and sea months ago, the prospect of stopping the mighty fleet the Americans had built was more than unlikely, it was to most Japanese admirals impossible.

To stop the invasion the Japanese navy relied on an old friend, deception. The plan for the contesting of the Philippine invasion was called the SHO-1 plan. (There was a SHO-2 and a SHO-3 plan but they were plans that dealt with invasions of other places.) In the SHO-1 plan the IJN split itself into three forces: the Northern Force, the Southern Force, the Center Force. The IJN Carriers were the Northern Force. They, along with two hybrid battleship-carriers, had been stationed in the home islands desperately trying to train carrier pilots after the disaster of the Battle of the Philippine Sea which had virtually gutted the IJN's carriers of pilots. The other forces, Southern and Center, were near the oil supply, south of the Philippines.

Simply put, in the SHO-1 plan, the carriers would "Show themselves" north of the Leyte beaches in an attempt to lure the US main force into to chasing them. Meanwhile, the IJN's remaining battleships would execute a pincer flank attack from either side of Leyte Gulf. Two battleships and their supports from Surigao Strait (the Southern Force,) and five battleships, including the mighty *Yamato* and *Musashi* (the largest battleships ever built) and significant supports from the San Bernandino Strait (the Center Force.) If they timed things right, the IJN carriers would show themselves so as to lure the 3rd fleet north before the other forces could be spotted. Things did not work out exactly that way.

FORMING TASK 34

On October 24 1944 at 1713 hours Admiral W. Lee, commander of the designated (but not formed) Task Force 34, received orders relative to the composition of his projected task force from Admiral Halsey. He was directed to concentrate in the area of the San Bernardino Straits.

As his units were part Task Forces 38.2 & 38.4 (both fast carrier task groups), which were also directed to concentrate in that area, the order was merely a formality. Heavy Japanese fleet units (the SHO plan's Center Force, or First Striking Force) had been sighted earlier in the day, headed for the San Bernardino Strait. This strategic waterway would lead the forces of the Japanese Navy right into the U.S. invasion forces off Leyte Gulf. But the Japanese had turned around, after first submarine and then air strikes had heavily damaged two heavy cruisers (forcing them to retire from the battle) and two battleships (not critically), and sank two heavy cruisers and the super battleship *Musashi*. In addition, several destroyers had been detached from the force to assist the damaged and sinking cruisers and BB *Musashi*.

Figure 1. *Musashi* down at the bow after air attack, October 24, 1944.

While the Task Force 34 assignment was merely precautionary, it had been announced as a contingency against just such an attempt by the Japanese. Orders took Task Forces 38.2 & 38.4 north at 2010 hours that same night, and the elements of Task Force 34 with it.

Just after dawn the following day the Japanese Center Force (4 BB, 6 CA, 2 CL, 10 DD remaining), which had again reversed course and transited San Bernardino Strait, fell upon elements of the U.S. escort carrier support groups in Leyte Gulf, precipitating the battle off Samar Island. 5 CVEs, 3 DDs and 3 DEs fought the Japanese so desperately that they disengaged and retreated, but not before the IJN sank 1 CVE, 2 DDs and 1 DE.

Since that day historians have continually attacked the reputation of Admiral Halsey for never actually forming Task Force 34 and leaving it to cover the invasion forces. Halsey's mistake at Leyte has been a common counter to anyone asserting Halsey was a great combat tactician. This decision not to leave a powerful surface force to block the San Bernardino Strait has become the most widely debated choice of his entire career.

Curiously, what this author has never seen discussed is what would have happened had Halsey implemented TF 34. Or, more to the point, what would have happened if the Japanese center force had actually collided with American fast battleships when it came out of the strait off Samar?

I suppose that the conventional wisdom would be that the American force would have quickly defeated the Japanese force. Or perhaps more simply, Task Force 34 would have stopped the Center Force. Well, the truth is, that isn't so certain. The battle, if it had occurred, would have been a very close run contest.

So what would have happened? Would the two combatants have actually engaged or would one have turned and fled? Who would have been surprised? It is well known that at the time that the USN had almost complete air supremacy; the Japanese were well aware of this and initiated the huge SHO-1 operation (of which the center force was a part) in spite of the expected air opposition.

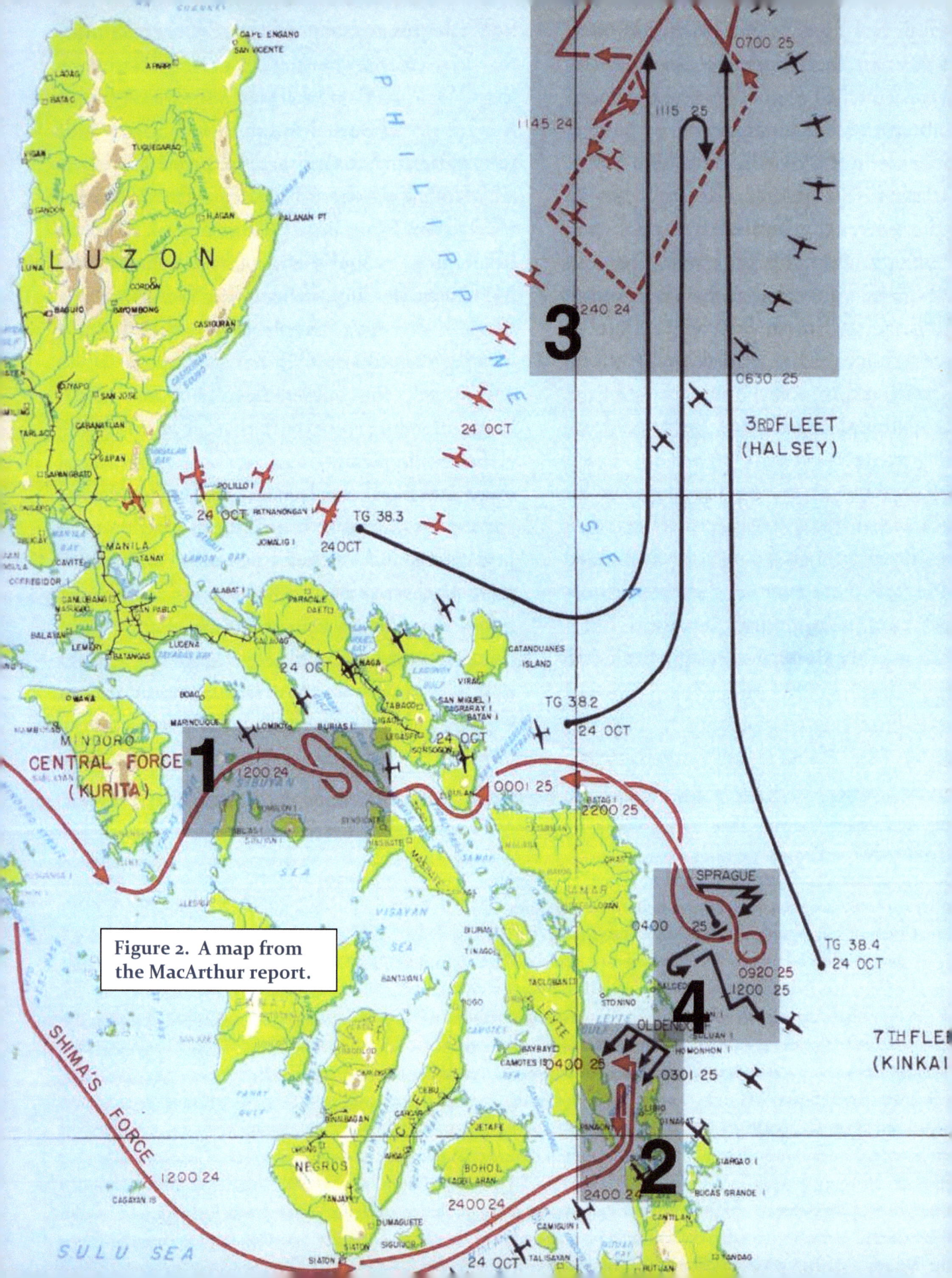

Figure 2. A map from the MacArthur report.

Yet even good intelligence gets ignored. Several times during the late hours of the 24th, Allied intelligence assets spotted the Japanese in the San Bernardino Strait. More than once messages were sent to Halsey in regards to the sightings, but for whatever reason he pressed on in pursuit of the elusive Japanese carriers to the north. One thing seems certain: if Halsey had detached Task Force 34 to block the strait, they would have met the Center Force.

In the real battle off Samar one could say that Kurita (the Japanese commander of the Center Force) became timid. He allowed those things that he thought were "going to happen" to become primary influences on what he thought was happening. And who could blame him? He had virtually no intelligence and he could only speculate as to how the US commander Halsey would react to his presence.

Surely a massive US fleet was nearby. It didn't seem possible that the entire offensive strike force of the US fleet had been lured away. Poor communications, no communications, the previous day's air strikes, and his lack of confidence in the plan all daunted him into believing that which was happening wasn't what it actually was. The whole point of the plan was to achieve exactly what it had in fact accomplished, but Kurita did not believe his own success.

The Japanese believed that the Americans would never divide their forces in front of their enemy, which is a military axiom, and intended to use this as the crux of their plan. Ironically, the US responded as expected at least partially. Because even though they both flew the same flag, there were really two US navies at Leyte: the Third Fleet commanded by Admiral Halsey (who reported to Admiral Nimitz), and the Seventh Fleet commanded by Admiral Kinkaid (who reported to General McArthur).

So one could say that the US had divided their forces, which allowed the decisive defeat of the Japanese Southern Force in Surigao Strait, and the pursuit of the Northern (or decoy) force. And yet neither fleet commander (Kinkaid nor Halsey) had divided *their* forces.

But this left the opening for the third Japanese (Center) force to succeed. Which for once vindicated the Japanese penchant for laboriously complex battle plans predicated on decoy tactics. Had Halsey realized that the

Northern Force was a decoy, or let the blocking force stay in position, the question becomes whether the two forces would have fought it out or, retreated in the face of powerful enemy units.

An analysis of battleship versus battleship encounters in World War II suggests that, more often than not, one side "chickened out" early on because they felt they were at some disadvantage. In those engagements that were fought through to a clear-cut decision, it can be argued that one of the fleets was unable to disengage even though they wanted to. In fact, only by unintentional cooperation by the enemy force were most surface fights ended. The side that was winning usually regrouped, ceased fire to make sure they weren't shooting at their own ships, made to open sea to continue their mission, or got timid.

In the case of the action off Samar, the answer to the question of mutual engagement seems fairly straightforward. The Japanese forces were already committed to a high-risk attack, almost suicidal in the minds of the commanding admirals. Although post war interviews with Kurita's frequently found him elusive or not willing to talk at all, the preponderance of the evidence suggests that they were obliged to take on whatever they encountered. They were, in fact, expecting heavy units of the US fleet. When Kurita discovered that the force in front of them was composed of aircraft carriers, he was sufficiently overjoyed that he sent headquarters a message saying BY HEAVEN-SENT OPPORTUNITY WE ARE DASHING TO ATTACK THE ENEMY CARRIERS – which was probably his way of saying "we got lucky." (They thought fleet carriers at the time, even though they were actually only escort carriers.)

The only way one could conceive of Kurita turning tail would be if he felt hopelessly out numbered. Since the two task forces were very evenly matched, one has to conclude that Kurita would have at least opened an engagement.

The American position was even more desperate. Lee would have little choice but to engage Kurita and his force. Retreating to wait for air support from the American fast carriers that were out of range would doom the escort carriers and possibly the invasion fleet to destruction. So it appears to this writer that both forces would have engaged, and probably stay engaged until one felt that they could not continue.

So what would happen then? Who would win? Well that is the whole point of this work. Listed below are the combatants of both fleets. The forces available for TF 34 are those that were designated in Halsey's dispatch to Lee at 1713 hrs, composed of ships from TF 38.2 & 38.4. I have read other authors who concluded that the force would have included all six of the Third Fleet's fast battleships. But I have not been able to find documentary evidence of that. I have seen a rendition of Lee's after action report, which quotes his orders of 1713hrs. Hence the battle order below.

THE OPPOSING FORCES

One has to appreciate the irony that with all the calculated decisions by higher authorities, chance happenings and engagements along the way, that force compositions would come out so closely matched. Both sides had four battleships, the Japanese had eight cruisers to the Americans' five, and the US carried the edge in destroyers by 14 to 11.

Composition of Task Force 34 (4 BB, 2 CA, 3 CL, 14 DD)

BB 56 - *Washington*
BB 60 - *Alabama*
BB 62 - *New Jersey*
BB 61 - *Iowa*
CA 45 - *Wichita*
CA 32 - *New Orleans*
CL 64 - *Vincennes*
CL 89 - *Miami*
CL 80 - *Biloxi*
DD 539 - *Tingey*
DD 536 - *Owen*
DD 535 - *Miller*
DD 537 - *The Sullivans*
DD 673 - *Hickox*
DD 674 - *Hunt*
DD 675 - *Lewis Hancock*
DD 676 - *Marshall*
DD 651 - *Cogswell*
DD 650 - *Caperton*

DD 652 - *Ingersoll*
DD 653 - *Knapp*
DD 392 - *Patterson*
DD 386 – *Bagley*

Figure 3. U.S.S. *New Jersey*, BB-62, at sea in the Pacific, 1944.

Composition of Center Force (4 BB, 6 CA, 2 CL, 11 DD)

BB *Yamato*
BB *Nagato* (slowed by earlier torpedo damage)
BB *Kongo*
BB *Haruna*
CA *Haurao*
CA *Chokai*
CA *Kumano*
CA *Suzuya*
CA *Tone*
CA *Chikuma*
CL *Noshiro*
CL *Yahagi*

DD *Fujinami*
DD *Urakaze*
DD *Kishinami*
DD *Isokaze*
DD *Okinami*
DD *Yukikaze*
DD *Hamanami*
DD *Nowaki*
DD *Hayashimo*
DD *Akishimo*
DD *Shimikaze*

Let's do the math first:

Figure 4. Ship Tonnage

US	317,999
Japanese	320,948

Figure 5. Broadside weight per minute in tons (total all ships with rate of fire included).

US	160.68
Japanese	114.45

Figure 6. Torpedoes

	Diameter	Number	Range (yards)	Warhead (pounds)	Total explosive (pounds)
US	21"	152	6,000	825	125,000
Japanese	24"	183	16,400	1,720	314,760

So what does the math say? U.S. and Japanese forces were very closely matched in tonnage. The US had a 40% advantage in shell weight by volume, mainly because of higher rates of fire, but there is a huge disparity in torpedoes in Japan's favor. Yet in the actual battle only the US employed their torpedoes (of which the escorts off Samar had 45 total) with any degree of success.

What can we tell from the cold statistical analysis? That the US could sit back and hammer the Japanese fleet to pieces long before they got in torpedo range? I think not.

Figure 7. A Japanese Type 93 "Long Lance" torpedo on display outside U.S. Navy headquarters, Washington, during World War II.

Even if the Japanese waited to launch torpedoes at shorter range (12,000 yards) the normal American practice would have been to close the range, and thereby give the enemy their opportunity. Even without this "close with the enemy" proclivity, the battle would have been coming at the U.S. task force, and retreating would have exposed the escort carriers and transports.

So, employed effectively, there is every possibility Japanese torpedoes could have been devastating (as they were early on in the war.) Perhaps more devastating than the imbalance in shell weight.

So has the math revealed anything? Perhaps it has shown that there is no easy answer. I don't believe that simple math works. One has to look elsewhere to decide who, if anyone, had the force advantage.

Ship by ship comparisons are another method that could be used to determine who might win such a battle. The American ships in this battle were generally newer, more technologically advanced, and faster. None of them had unrepaired battle damage as did several of the Japanese ships (notably the *Nagato* & *Yamato*.) While their damage did not in any way affect their armament, it did affect their sea keeping, speed and endurance.

Figure 8. *Yamato* during trials, 1941.

Figure 9. U.S.S. *Iowa*, BB-61, at sea 1944.

Various sources have generally speculated about the U.S. advantages in armor quality, ammunition fusing, and radar fire control, all of which would have figured greatly in any set piece surface battle. The Japanese had the best optical range finding gear ever made on the *Yamato*. However, there can be little doubt that escort forces making smoke would have complicated and degraded the Japanese optical advantage shortly after the steel started flying.

Any comparison of ship versus ship combat in this engagement (and one of the chief reasons for my inviting this discussion) stimulates the "who would win an *Iowa* versus *Yamato* battle?" argument. Most Western historians give the *Iowa* an edge in such a battle. (I have to admit to never reading Japanese replies or arguments along these lines.)

The edge, as I understand it, lies mainly with radar fire control, better quality of ammunition, and better construction (armor and quality of building). In my estimation, other than the radar fire control, these intangible "betters" are at best questionable.

The alleged superior quality of *Iowa's* armor is certainly countered by the *Yamato's* undoubtedly much thicker armor (12.1" belt and 6" deck Vs 16.1" belt and 9" deck). Debate still rages about the relative merits of the *Iowa's* 16"/50 gun versus the *Yamato's* 18.1"/45, with some postwar studies giving an edge to the 16"/50 in penetrating power. *Iowa's* armor provided an immune zone of only 5300 yards against her own 2700 pound AP shell, and there can be little confidence in the existence of any immune zone against *Yamato's* 3200 pound AP shell. It is the question of who got the first effective hit that by far out-weighs the theoretical question of which ship had better armor or guns since both classes were extremely heavily armed and hits were likely to do great damage. And *Yamato's* 18.1" guns did throw a heavier AP shell than *Iowa's* 16" guns. *Iowa* did enjoy a substantial speed advantage (33 knots Vs 27 knots).

Of course the other problem with "who is better, *Iowa* or *Yamato*" is that this isn't a one on one battle. There is no guarantee that either ship would fire on the other.

Consequently, after assigning the proper weight to the *Yamato's* contribution, a U.S. battleship advantage becomes apparent. The *Nagato* was a dominant ship when she was built in the 1920s, probably ahead of British and American designs of the time. But, although she remained a formidable adversary, she was outclassed by the more modern battleship designs by 1944.

Unfortunately for her, four of the ships that outclassed her were in the opposing force. Her 16.1"/45 guns were good, and for the most part a match for the American 16"/45. But her fire control system, and probably her armor, was inferior. Her speed was somewhat less than her adversaries (26 knots compared to 27 knots for *Alabama* and *Washington* and 33 knots for *Iowa* and *New Jersey*), magnified by carrying torpedo damage into battle. On her very best day, on paper, *Nagato* might have given *Washington* a pretty hard time.

The *Kongo* and *Haruna* were near the bottom limit of ships that could be considered battleships at all. They were designed and built as WW I battle cruisers (very similar to the British *Repulse* and *Renown*) and upgraded to "battleship" status during the 1930's. Many postulate that they were more properly classed as battle cruisers since their armor scheme and thickness was suspect. Their 14" guns and older fire control equipment made them less effective than any of the U.S. battleships of Task Force 34. All of the U.S. battleships had a useful immune zone against the *Kongo's* 14" guns. The *Kongos* were, however, at 30 knots faster than all of the other capital ships involved except for the *Iowas*.

This is not to say they were worthless ships, far from it, but they were not a proper choice for a battleship versus battleship confrontation. Witness the *Hiei's* bad treatment in the first naval battle of Guadalcanal on 13 August 42 when she was overcome by 8" & 5" shell fire. A properly armored battleship might have suffered casualties and damage from such fire, but would not have been as heavily damaged as she was.

On the other hand, in the close range night battle known as the 2nd Battle of Guadalcanal, *Kirishima* and accompanying cruisers quickly knocked *South Dakota*, sister of *Alabama*, out of the fight. Minutes later *Kirishima* was herself blindsided by *Washington* and mortally wounded. Such are the vagaries of real capital ship encounters.

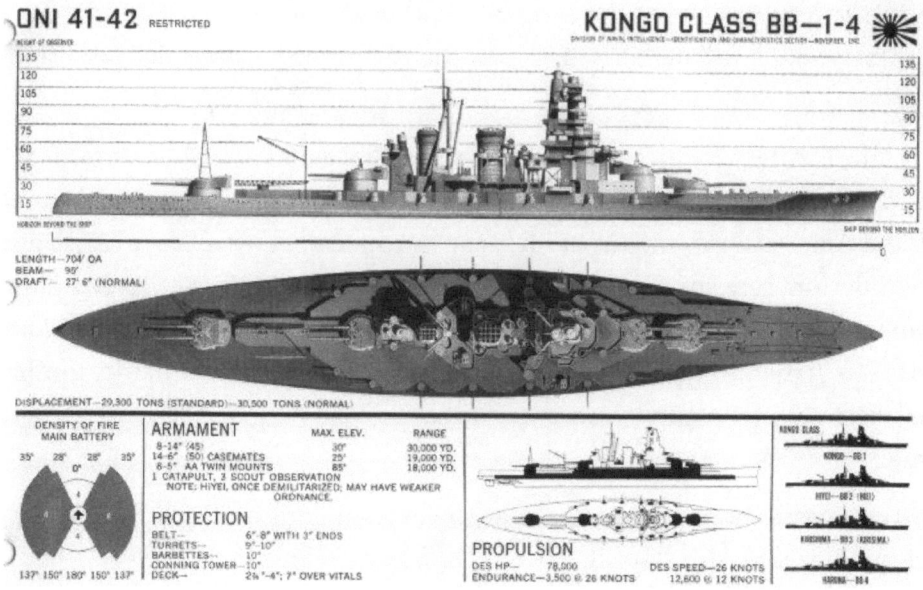

Figure 10. Office of Naval Intelligence profile of *Kongo* and *Haruna*, 1941.

Figure 11. U.S.S. *Washington*, BB-56, 1944.

So in the realm of how the battleships would have fared in this fight, it seems likely that had these combatants been left to slug it out amongst themselves the *Iowa, New Jersey, Washington* and *Alabama* would probably have prevailed against the *Yamato, Nagato, Kongo* and *Haruna*.

The cruiser versus cruiser analysis is a much closer and more abstract argument. The Japanese had advantages in tonnage, torpedoes, and many more heavy gun barrels. Yet the Americans had faster firing, radar guided guns of (for the most part) smaller bore.

I have to comment on this. Japanese heavy cruisers were handsome ships, well designed aesthetically and practically conceived. They presented an image of majesty and power under way. That they mightily fudged the naval treaty tonnage limits was to their credit by this time in the war. Looking out a pair of high-powered binoculars and seeing six of these beauties heading your way in line abreast would have been the source of severe indigestion to an American cruiser skipper.

Figure 12. Heavy cruiser *Chikuma* inducing indigestion in U.S. skippers.

In the end, although I have no doubt the U.S. cruisers would have acquitted themselves well in any surface engagement. I have to say that in terms of cruisers versus cruisers the Japanese force was much stronger. Without aid from their battleship or destroyer cousins, the U.S. cruisers would mostly likely have lost.

As to destroyer versus destroyer comparisons the US *Fletchers* (of which 12 of the 14 American destroyers were) had pretty well proven more than a match for the Japanese destroyers, with perhaps the exception of the *Shimikaze*. In terms of construction and ability to absorb damage, the *Fletchers* were extraordinary vessels and their fire output and accuracy was an order of magnitude better than any of the Japanese destroyers. Twelve of them should have more than been able to handle the eleven Japanese ships.

Figure 13. Destroyer *Shimakaze*, 1943.

Now I realize this sounds like I am saying that the Japanese torpedoes would have no effect on the battle. I am not. What I am saying is that a Japanese destroyer hit by the lesser power American 21" torpedo was just as likely to be disabled as an American destroyer struck by the powerful 24" Japanese torpedo.

My contention is that superior American damage control and construction was more obvious in the smaller ships built than the larger, and hence would be a more telling factor in the smaller combatants. Simply put, one torpedo would not likely put the *Yamato* or *Iowa* out of action, even if Iowa were more affected by the hit than the *Yamato*. (Likely given the record of the *Yamato* class for absorbing torpedo damage.) However, one torpedo may be more than enough to put a destroyer out of action and thus the degree to which the damage could be controlled would be much more relevant to keeping the ship afloat.

Figure 14. U.S.S. *Fletcher*, DD-445, underway off New York, 1942.

The tenor of the three arguments here tends to favor the Americans. The Japanese only advantage is in the cruiser versus cruiser match up. But remember, I postulated one thing in the beginning of the *Iowa* Vs *Yamato* argument that I think carries through the entire flow of discussion. It's not so much whether you have a bigger, faster firing, or more accurate gun than the other guy, it's whether in this particular time and place you get the first good hit. If the *Yamato* scores early on the *Iowa*, the *Yamato* becomes the favorite, and vice versa. It is the same for the *Kongo* firing on the *New Jersey*. Sure, she has less penetrating power, but if she gets that "lucky" hit, the whole battle could change.

Consider the 2nd battle of Guadalcanal 14 November 1942. The *South Dakota* takes an early 14" hit from the *Kirishima*, which knocks out her power distribution, disabling her fire control, and sends the ship into darkness. For several minutes she was a punching bag for much of the Japanese task force as she was silhouetted in front of a burning ship. Had the *Washington* not been there to blast away at the *Kirishima* and put her out of the fight, things might have gone very badly for *South Dakota*, all because of one early critical hit. (Note: I realize that this is an oversimplification and that other factors contributed to this, such as the chief engineer using tape to hold circuit breakers closed. But the initial hit bears directly on the result, regardless of mitigating factors.) Simply said, the side that hits first gains an advantage, and it can reverse an imbalance.

So my belief, using any of these comparison types of arguments whether by math or individual ship value, is that while the Americans may have some advantage, the edge is actually too close to call. However, I will weigh in on a factor that I think would have been decisive had the battle been prosecuted to a conclusion. That factor is training.

Now I am not saying that one side had better trained sailors than the other. In fact, I believe that in some ways Japanese sailors were better trained. In this instance the training I am referring to is tactical training. By this time in the war the Imperial Japanese Navy was no longer engaging in real training exercises. This was mainly due to fuel shortages and the submarine threat. The US Navy was training at every opportunity, especially if they were expecting battle or were a part of a newly formed unit. This was a luxury afforded by the abundance of supply they enjoyed, freedom of navigation (especially in rear areas), and their much better ship availability situation, which actually allowed extensive times for post repair/refit work-up and pre-engagement practice maneuvers.

Believe it or not, and this is my conjecture (not something I am quoting), the disparity of readiness between the two forces was in my estimation the greatest important difference. In short, the Americans would have been better prepared to fight a surface action than the Japanese. Even though the Japanese were the ones challenging battle!

One of my chief reasons for my above hypothesis is the fact that Kurita never really put forward a battle plan. Even though most battle plans don't survive much after first contact, they do give all of the participants a level of expectation and general indicators of responsibilities and contingencies. Admiral Lee would certainly have laid out such a plan.

Kurita called for a "General" engagement in the actual battle. One disappointing aspect of his approach was his decision to position his destroyers at the rear of the column, cutting his advantage in torpedoes severely, or at least delaying its arrival into the battle. Even more telling was his lack of attempts to control the battle once it commenced. There was no order to concentrate fire, or prepare for torpedo attacks.

This is not to say that the Japanese ship captains were inept. Individually they pursued the Americans like hungry tigers. But there was very little cooperation between them.

THE BATTLE

So, just to go one step farther, this is the way I see the battle taking shape. Since we already know how Kurita proceeded, I will at first speak to Lee's plan and Kurita's reactions.

First, if Lee was left to guard the Strait, then he would have guarded it. It is not reasonable to assume that the first American sight of approaching enemy battleships would have been a warning from an anti-submarine patrolling TBF, as actually occurred. Much more likely would be a screen of eight to ten destroyers in the Strait, which would have had instructions along these lines: "If enemy force is sighted, notify the fleet, illuminate, and engage." These ships however would not have been placed so far down the Strait as to be out of the range of the heavier ships of TF 34.

How Kurita would have reacted to a force of American destroyers engaging him with guns and torpedoes in the early morning is not an easy call. Certainly his cruisers and destroyers would have responded immediately. My guess is he would have pressed on until or unless battle damage compelled him to retire. I think it is a certainty that some US destroyer success would have been achieved. And by this I mean that while the destroyers would have taken losses, perhaps initially heavy, they would have scored some hits on Kurita's battle line. How many and how serious the hits would have guided any decision by Kurita to withdraw.

The heat and confusion of battle being what it is, my conclusion is that he would have most likely continued; at least to the point of sighting and engaging the US heavy units. At that point, the aforementioned theory of who fires first and who hits first becomes the guiding principal of how the engagement would proceed.

To begin with, Lee would likely have enjoyed an huge initial advantage of lazily sailing back and forth in the southwestern mouth of the Strait with his cruisers and battleships effectively gaining a "Crossing the T" position at the start. Of course, Kurita and his captains would maneuver to bring all their guns into play once the opening salvos were received, but I can't imagine the American radar advantage coupled with the warning the destroyers would provide not giving them the first shots. My thoughts are that US cruisers would have been at about 12,000 yards and BBs 16-18,000 when they opened fire.

At that range in the early dawn, it is unlikely that Kurita would even know who was shooting at him. Their initial return fire would be at the flashes of the American guns, which would probably first mean the American cruisers. For a short time the US cruisers would probably be receiving 14"-18" shell fire from the Japanese BBs.

Once again, the hit equation comes into play. One hit on a *Cleveland* Class cruiser by a battleship shell would be no small problem. The *Clevelands* would begin blasting away, their battle plan attempting to pick out the enemy cruisers and destroyers, with some degree of success. The same could be said of the American heavy cruisers, albeit at slower rates, and they might well engage the Japanese BBs, the largest available targets.

In the Surigao Strait battle, radar equipped U.S. BBs actually had their radars masked at times by the cruiser column a few thousand yards ahead of them. So the American BBs would fire, but would occasionally be compelled to cease-fire because their radar picture would become confused. Since this is early dawn, optics would be of lesser value even with star shell illumination. At first, when the *Iowa, New Jersey, Alabama* and *Washington* commenced firing, they would have had a huge accuracy advantage.

Task Force 34's Moment of Glory

Figure 15. U.S.S. *Alabama*, BB-60, December 1942.

It is when the hits began, and then started to mount, that Kurita would have most likely made a fateful decision to disengage. Of course, the problem with this is that his battleships were generally slower than their US counterparts. Lee would not likely have disengaged until he began to run low on ammunition or lost ships. I am unaware of how much AP (armor piercing) ammo that typically was loaded out on a US battleship, but their magazine capacity was around 100 rounds per barrel. I am guessing that 60-70% of these would be the AP kind since you can still shoot AP for shore bombardment where you can't really engage an enemy battleship with HE (high explosive) rounds. So it makes sense to carry the majority for a fight you can't afford to lose.

THE OPENING ROUNDS

If the U.S. battleships crossed the Japanese "T" the leading Japanese heavy unit would draw the combined fire of all four US Battleships. If that ship were *Yamato*, even she, assuming that she hadn't taken any additional torpedo hits from US destroyers in the Strait, couldn't have withstood that kind of pounding for long. *Washington* hit *Kirishima* with 9 rounds out of 75 (12%) fired in a confused night action off Guadalcanal in 1942. The engagement was at closer ranges, but it was in full darkness with older radar.

Even if you take into consideration greater range, you also have to factor in that the main advantage of crossing the "T" lies in the greater probability of a hit. But just for argument's sake we will put U.S. accuracy down to 5%. One out of every twenty rounds fired hits the *Yamato*. The U.S. BBs can fire two rounds a minute, but remember we said they'd be masked occasionally, so we will compute for 1.5 rounds per minute. That's 36 barrels at 1.5 rounds per minute, which works out to 54 rounds per minute or slightly less than three hits per minute!

So, three 2700-pound shells per minute would slam into the *Yamato*. One can only surmise how long the *Yamato*, as great as she was, could last. Certainly no more than ten minutes.

On the receiving end for the U.S., I can't possible believe that the Japanese would be able to achieve the same level of fire coordination. I say this because there was no real battle plan, they had no real way of identifying targets, and the Japanese had a much less effective way of targeting them in the semi-darkness. One has to assume they would have fired star shells, and maneuvered to unmask their guns. This would have partially removed the crossed "T" effect. Yet still, one could only conclude that the Japanese BBs would end up firing piecemeal.

No doubt by coincidence this would involve one or two, possibly even three ending up firing on the same ship, but this might not last as they could lose sight of their target in the smoke and confusion of battle. Yet in order to construct an understandable flow here, I am going to assume some degree of coordination.

The *Yamato* was said to be able to fire 1.5 rounds per minute per barrel. I think that's a little optimistic, but for the purposes of this discussion, we need to consider the professionalism, and perhaps desperation, of the crews. The Japanese accuracy at moderate to long range was not that great in any engagement of the war. In the Battle of the Java Sea on February 27 1942, at ranges from 16 to 20,000 yards the Japanese heavy cruisers fired collectively 1,819 8" shells for five hits! Of course the two Allied heavy cruisers involved scored only one hit in several hundred rounds fired. So being as optimistic as possible let's assume an accuracy of 2.5% or half that of the radar guided U.S. guns.

This means in ten minutes of firing (135 rounds if all guns remained serviceable) the *Yamato* would score three hits. We will tally one of them on say the *New Orleans*, which, as we said would be a likely first target. The *Nagato* and the *Kongos* had slightly higher firing rates, which were around two rounds per minute. If the *Nagato* and *Kongo* were both engaging (let's say the *Iowa*) in ten minutes she might be struck by two 18" rounds, three 16" rounds and four 14" rounds, probably knocking her out of the battle, although not sinking her. We are going to give the *Vincennes* a hit by a 16" and a hit by a 14" projectile, instead of the *Iowa*, which accounts for the initial confusion we spoke of earlier, knocking *Vincennes* out of the battle, but watching *Iowa* to see if she's still in it.

Even if *Haruna*, the other Japanese battleship, managed to target the *New Jersey*, *Washington* or *Alabama*, she could at best hit her with five 14" rounds (leaving out the temporary shooting at a cruiser for one battleship.) Those rounds probably wouldn't have a decisive effect on, say, *Alabama*, but might well reduce her speed, reduce her secondary and AA battery by 30%, and force her to switch to her aft main battery fire control station due to battle damage. We can safely assume that the Japanese battleship shell hits did some quality damage to one of the US BBs, almost disabling one (*Iowa*) and damaging another (*Alabama*). After ten minutes of engagement Kurita (assuming he is still alive) might perhaps have sized up his situation something like this:

> *We have engaged major units of the enemy fleet including battleships, cruisers and destroyers while exiting San Bernardino Strait. Aboard the* Yamato, *much is in disarray. We are slowed to 15 knots, taking on water, and afire amidships. I have learned though that the rest of the battleships are still relatively undamaged save for some hits to the* Haruna *(errant US 8" targeting). The* Yamato *is slowing and turning out of line. If we can make progress on the fires, we will return to the battle. The cruisers are now charging our adversaries, as are the remaining destroyers. We have lost three of our heavy cruisers, one of our light cruisers, and three of our destroyers to the enemy destroyer ambush. In return we have achieved a glorious victory over them as eight of them are burning and drifting in the Strait. I propose to continue on to our heaven-*

sent opportunity against the enemy invasion fleet. I have not had communication with the northern or southern forces and can only assume they have proceeded with their missions successfully. I hope to meet Admiral Nishimura off Leyte.

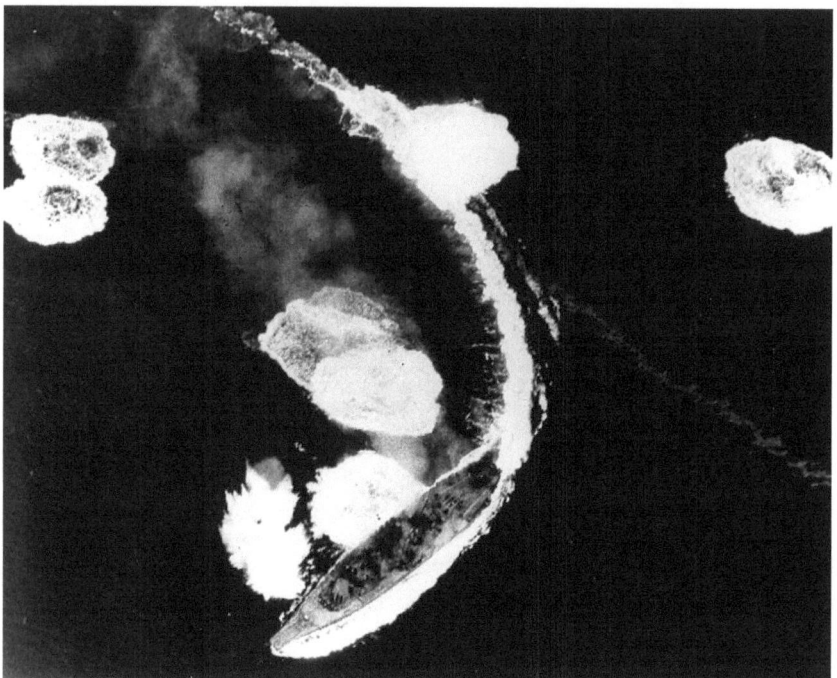

Figure 16. *Yamato* under air attack, 1945.

THE BATTLE CONTINUES

With the *Yamato* turning out of line, US targeting becomes less certain. Her being afire would guarantee some continued attention. But my guess is that at least two of the U.S. BBs would shift fire to the next large target, yet that's not a simple decision. After the *Yamato*, the other three Japanese battleships have nearly the same dimensions, and on such an inexact thing as a radar scope, you probably could not tell the difference between a *Nagato* and a *Kongo*. Most likely it would instead be the closest ship, which would be the *Haruna* since before engagement the Japanese battleships had been steaming in twin columns, *Yamato* and *Haruna* in the lead of their respective pairings.

As we said before, there is a prospect of a "lucky hit" to be accounted for, so take one of the U.S. BBs out of the fight due to battle damage. After 10 minutes of firing an 18" shell penetrates the *Iowa's* side armor and rips through one of the engine rooms slicing through a critical section of power cable in the process and putting the brakes on her speed and ability to fire. Heroic damage control parties leap into action, but it will be 20 minutes to restore enough power to operate her radar and guns. Listing, she shears out of line and begins to open the range. The *New Jersey* continues to fire at *Yamato* for five more minutes, scoring four more hits, which leaves *Washington* and *Alabama* to take *Haruna* under fire. In those tragic five minutes aboard the *Haruna* we would see her rocked with ten hits.

We know that nine such hits just about did in her sister in 1942. The Japanese answer back as best they can, but the fire from the *Yamato* and *Haruna* has been cut in half during the short 300 seconds. *Iowa* suffers one more (non-critical) 18" hit, while *Alabama* comes in for three 14" and two 16" hits. She shears out of formation and out of the battle. Prompt and efficient damage control will save the ship, but she will have to return to Pearl Harbor for temporary repairs and San Francisco for full repair.

Kurita, communications now out, looks out his shattered flag bridge window, to see the once proud and powerful *Haruna* in flames slowly turning in circles, two of her turrets still firing in local control. His own ship, the *Yamato*, has suffered more: one of her huge main turrets has been jammed by damage, water is rushing in and the ship is significantly down by the bow, and she has been reduced to a much lower rate of fire by electrical failures. Her survival is in question. Off in the distance he can see three enemy ships on fire, and two battleships turning away from the battle.

His cruisers (two more of which are on fire and slowing) and destroyers have just loosed several dozen torpedoes at the enemy. He has still not heard from either the northern or southern forces. He is in grim awe of the power of the enemy ships, which are rending the cream of the Japanese Navy. As daylight brightens, he also faces the prospect of an entire day of what surely must be imminent enemy air attack. There is now little hope that, even if he defeated the force he is now facing, he will have sufficient force left to carry through to the vulnerable invasion areas. All things considered, he decides to save what he can of the fleet. He takes advantage of this chance that the enemy will have to turn away to evade the approaching torpedoes, and hoists the "General Retreat" flag.

THE CRUISER AND DESTROYER BATTLE

Up until now, the six Japanese heavy cruisers have been engaging the American heavy and light cruisers. Over 30-8" and 1-18" shells as well as a couple dozen 5" shells have struck the *New Orleans*. She is sinking, a flaming wreck.

The *Vincennes* has been hit by over 30-8", a couple dozen 5", as well as two major caliber hits from the battleships, and she too is sinking. The *Wichita* is the victim of somewhere between 15 and 20-8" hits, a dozen or so 5" hits, and while still firing one of her turrets, she is combat ineffective other than as a target to split the rain of Japanese shells. The *Miami* and *Biloxi* have absorbed several 5" hits, but are continuing to fire at any Japanese cruisers and destroyers in range.

The Japanese cruisers have suffered as well. The *Cumana* and *Chikuma* are early torpedo victims, but are able at the start of the battle to severely maul a couple destroyers and then trade salvos with the US cruisers. The *Haurao* and *Tone* become the first targets of the light cruisers, while the *Kumana* and *Chikuma* get the 8" fire from *Wichita* and *New Orleans*.

The US switched from deploying heavy cruisers to light cruisers in situations likely to produce surface actions because of one thing: rate of fire. A US heavy cruiser could fire 3 to 4 rounds per minute per barrel while a *Cleveland* class light cruiser could fire 8 to 10, and the *Clevelands* had 12 barrels instead of 9. So the math here (and there) wasn't that hard 36-260 pound shells a minute versus 120-105 pound shells or 9360 pounds versus 12600 pounds in shell weight. In point of fact, it is likely that the *Cleveland* class cruisers in this battle may be the only ships to actually run out of ammunition, since they carried 200 rounds per barrel and could possibly expend that in twenty minutes.

Figure 17. U.S.S. *Cleveland, CL-55,* under way late 1942.

But in that twenty minutes it is very likely that they achieve more than 360-6" hits on their adversaries. So when I mention the *Haurao* and *Tone* being the light cruisers first targets, it is very likely that those hits would be spread out over all of the Japanese cruisers involved (including the light cruisers) since the CLs would have shifted fire when the Japanese ships slowed or turned. The Japanese saw their CLs as destroyer leaders, and the *Toshiro* and *Yahagi* would have led the charge to torpedo launch points. In presenting themselves so, they would have been begging for a beating by the American CLs, whose task would have been to prevent such an obvious sortie.

After their successful launch of torpedoes the Japanese CLs and DDs would have turned away. Some would engage cripples, such as American DDs that were still trying to salvage themselves after being first in and first bloodied in the Strait, and some would add their fire against the American cruisers.

Figure 18. Battleship *Nagato*, from the George Grantham Bain collection at the Library of Congress.

LAST SALVOS

It would be several minutes before all the Japanese ships would see and obey the command to retire. During those next five minutes, the *Washington* continues to pound the *Haruna*, which receives five more hits leaving her a burning wreck. She is the second ship of that class *Washington* has defeated.

The *New Jersey* shifts to the *Nagato* scoring six times and opens up more of her hull to the sea, magnifying her earlier torpedo damage.

The *Haruna* never scores again. The *Yamato* continues sporadic fire in local control, but also is unsuccessful. *Nagato* still has *Alabama* in her sights and scores twice, while *Kongo* manages three more 14" hits on "*Bama*," which by now is in very bad shape.

From his lofty perch on the Flag Bridge of the unscathed *Washington*, Admiral Lee sees the battering the *Alabama* is taking. She is wrapped in flames abaft the stack, and slowing. He has a radio message in hand "CAPTAIN DEAD, REMAINING MAIN BATTERY IN LOCAL CONTROL, SPEED FIFTEEN KNOTS, ACTING CO BB ALABAMA" Lee can only shake his head and whisper his amazement of the bravery of the men on the ship a thousand yards away from him.

Two minutes later, as he watches the effect of *Washington* and *New Jersey* concentrating fire on the *Nagato*, he is shocked to see a roaring flash billow up the side of the *Miami* several thousand yards away, and moments after that the same scene occurs to the *Wichita*. Lee instantly realizes that the Japanese have launched their dreaded "Long Lance" torpedoes, and there is little doubt that several are headed his way. He quickly alerts the Captain, busy fighting his ship, who orders a 90-degree turn to starboard, which takes them away from the enemy.

But those previous two minutes are enough to seal *Nagato's* fate, hit by four more 16" shells, she suffers a hit to one of her engine rooms, slowing and setting her afire. *Kongo* has turned away now and only is firing her rear turrets. She does not score again.

It's ten long minutes before Lee is assured that he has successfully "combed" the torpedoes and can turn to reengage. His only remaining targets are crippled *Nagato*, the burning *Haruna*, a suffering *Kumano*, a limping

Suzuya, the smoldering hulk of *Yahagi*, and 3 lingering destroyers, which they make short work of. But it is now dawn, and the arrival of American escort carriers' air groups ends any hope of escape.

Yamato and *Kongo*, *Noshiro* and four DDs make it back through the straight, but the former, unable to increase her speed significantly after the battle, is sunk by waves of American planes before she can escape.

In the battle, the Americans lose the cruisers *New Orleans*, *Wichita*, *Miami* and *Vincennes* along with eight *Fletcher*-class destroyers. The battleships *Iowa* and *Alabama* are seriously damaged, eventually return Stateside for repair, but are effectively out of action for the remainder of the war.

The Japanese lose the battleships *Nagato*, *Haruna*, all of their cruisers save *Noshiro*, and all but 4 destroyers. The *Yamato* should properly be considered a victim of the battle, since it is finished by air attack the next day.

AFTERMATH

For the USN stopping the Japanese Center force was a costly surface battle, and yet the invasion fleet was successfully defended. The losses could be made good. For the IJN, on the other hand, the loss of the Battle of Leyte Gulf marks its end as a significant fighting force in the Second World War.

Certainly some immediate consequences of the battle would be a brief reexamination of the priority of the battleship as a national and naval asset by both nations. For the Japanese it would be a condemnation that their expensive investment over the long years prior to the war would have been much better spent on carriers. Conversely it is very likely that the success of the battle would draw rather a reaffirmation on the American side and catapult Admiral Willis Lee into a more prominent place in history.

The effects of ship losses would probably not affect the war's timeline of major events on either side. The Japanese would have one lone *Kongo* class ship left which would likely skulk around the home islands until it was caught by carrier planes. There were no battleships under construction by 1944 in Japan. They were struggling to replace their losses in carriers with little success. The American fleet could easily do without the services of the battleships seriously damaged in the battle; in fact they had two more *Iowa* class battleships commissioned in 1944, as well as a battle cruiser of the *Alaska* class. The refocus on the value of battleships however may have allowed one or two of the Iowa's never completed sisters, the *Illinois* and the *Kentucky*, to be completed since they were delayed during the war due to the perceived need for higher priority ships. The *Kentucky* was reported 73% complete when construction was halted on her.

Of course the *Yamato's* suicidal thrust toward Okinawa in April of 1945 would never had happened, and Ernest Evans would probably have survived the war never being award a Congressional Medal of Honor (Posthumously) for his gallant leadership of the *USS Johnston* off Samar in the real battle that occurred that day. Instead of one of the most lopsided battles ever fought, history would forever remember the battle as the last great battleship vs. battleship encounter; perhaps inspiring Jutland-like comparisons and examinations of shot placement and evasive maneuvering.

But probably the single biggest change in events afterward would have been how history viewed the careers of two naval leaders; one American and one Japanese. In reality the reputations of both Admiral Kurita, who led the Center Force, and Admiral Halsey who made the fateful decision not to deploy TF 34, suffered greatly from the orders they gave that day. Kurita was the leader who should have continued on and yet turned around and fled from a vastly inferior force fearing a larger one was coming. Halsey was guilty of a strategic blunder, leaving his flank unguarded and being tricked into pursuing enemy carriers that carried no planes.

It is very likely that, even in defeat, no shame would have been attributed to Kurita for losing to an American force such as TF 34. And there would have been no suggestion of blunder by Halsey in sending US battleships to meet him. Regardless of the casualties history would count both leaders among the most capable and courageous leaders of their nation, and in Kurita's case it probably would have earned him hero's status since he would have gone down with Yamato. As it was he lived out his life afterwards in obscurity, performing common labor, and refusing to talk about the war.

Halsey, who had been built up as a hero already by the American press and Navy public relations, went through the rest of his life having to defend his decision at Leyte. Every time he was lauded for his leadership in the war there was always the whisper of his failure at Leyte. It was the major blight in an otherwise brilliant career.

Imagine having that weight taken off of them. Each would have enjoyed a much better treatment after conflict. For Halsey perhaps a higher calling such as politics or Chief of Naval Operations... For Kurita an honorable and heroic death, which in the Japanese culture of the time was the ultimate achievement

Naval historians, frustrated by the history they are tied to, know that for a brief instant in time on the 24th of October 1944, there was a very real possibility of US and Japanese battleships coming to blows off Samar Island. For the benefit of those who endlessly speculate this book provides some foundation. It doesn't claim to be the end all, but rather the begin all.

A bitter irony of the battle is that, while unknown to the Japanese at the time, the prize they were after, the US invasion fleet sitting off Leyte, was largely empty. Sinking empty hulls would have had an effect, but it wouldn't have hurt the US war effort much. In the end, the engagement, had it been fought, would have proven little. Those that fought there and survived would have its memory and horrors stay with them for the rest of their lives. Those that died there would have been enshrined by grateful nations as heroes. But by October of 1944 the war had been decided, and the Japanese had no chance of reversing their fortune. Unlike other great battles, its outcome would have decided nothing.

BB-67 *Montana*, U.S. Navy Battleship: Why She Matters Today (also from Nimble Books)

This is one of my favorites in the ever-growing Nimble Books list. The cover looks terrific--very realistic, just as if the Navy had really built the U.S.S. *Montana*! The interior of the book includes:

- pictures and information about the various design concepts that were explored
- the specifications of the final *Montana* design
- color pictures of a beautiful 1:700 scale model of *Montana* by Imre Somogyi
- a beautiful color painting of *Montana* by author and artist Wayne Scarpaci
- a picture of her never-built 1920's predecessor, BB-51 *Montana*
- an essay on "Why She Matters Today"; and
- a discussion of Senator Jon Tester's efforts to get the U.S. Navy to name a capital ship after his home state of Montana.

In short, this presents a unique package of art and text devoted exclusively to one of the most interesting hypothetical ships ever designed.

It is available on Amazon.com.

COLOPHON

Webster's Revised Unabridged, copyright 1996, 1998, MICRA, Inc.:

> \Col"o*phon\ (k[o^]l"[-o]*f[o^]n), n. [L. colophon **finishing stroke,** Gr. kolofw`n; cf. L. culmen top, collis hill. Cf. Holm.] An inscription, monogram, or cipher, containing the place and date of publication, printer's name, etc., formerly placed on the last page of a book.

And, according to the American Heritage dictionary, Colophon was an ancient Greek city of Asia Minor northwest of Ephesus, which was famous for its cavalry.

The current usage of the colophon in the publishing industry is to describe the fonts used in the book. But I think this is wrong-headed: the last page in the book is too important to be devoted to technical minutiae. So I always like to find a substantive finishing stroke for each book that I publish.

In this case, what could be more appropriate than the (incorrectly decoded) message that Admiral Halsey received from Nimitz on 25 October as Admiral Kurita engaged Taffy 3?

TURKEY TROTS TO WATER GG FROM CINCPAC ACTION COM THIRD FLEET INFO COMINCH CTF SEVENTY-SEVEN X WHERE IS RPT WHERE IS TASK FORCE THIRTY FOUR RR THE WORLD WONDERS[1]

—Fred Zimmerman, Nimble Books LLC,
Ann Arbor, Michigan, USA, 2008

---

[1] As most TF 34 aficionados will recall, the first four and the last three words were padding added by cryptographers and were not intended to be part of the message.

www.ingramcontent.com/pod-product-compliance
Lightning Source LLC
Chambersburg PA
CBHW042019150426
43197CB00002B/80